CHINA

Few areas of the world are changing so
rapidly as mainland China while giving out
so little information to the rest of the world.
Other nations watch with great interest
and some concern the future of this
tremendous country.

With the aid of outstanding photographs,
drawings and maps the author of this book
helps the reader to find out what is
happening in China today. Especially he
describes the village communes, flood
control projects, industrial expansion,
railroads and shipping.

FINDING OUT ABOUT GEOGRAPHY

Art Editors Colin Banks & John Miles
Illustrations by Zena Flax

The John Day Company
New York

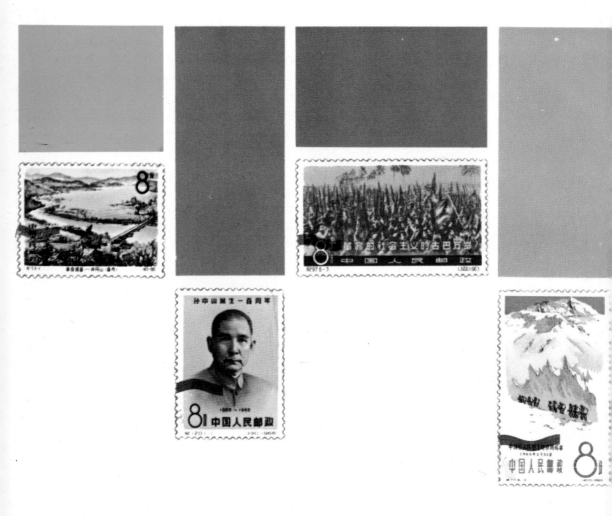

China

by Robert Clayton

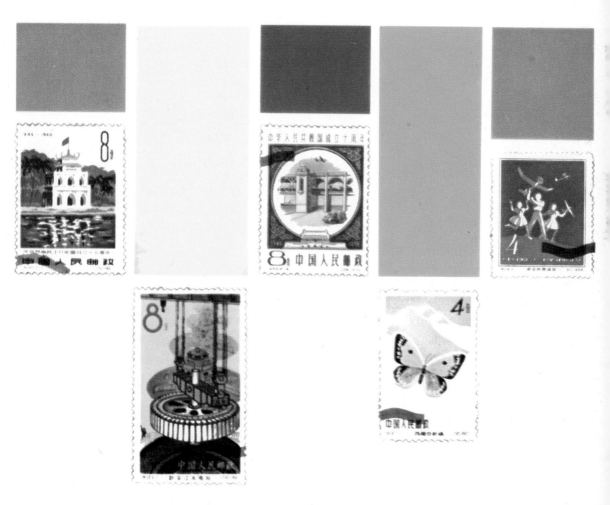

Photograph acknowledgments

China Photo Service: 14, 17 bis, 24, 25, 27, 28, 29, 30/31, 32, 33, 36, 37, 40

Hsinhua News Agency: 8, 12, 13

Radio Times Hulton Picture Library: 9

NCNA: 44, 45

United States Information Service: 41

The John Day Company, 257 Park Avenue South, New York, N.Y. 10010
an Intext publisher
Library of Congress Catalogue Card Number - 74—132951

Contents

China is one of the areas of the world where man was making great progress thousands of years ago. Thus it is that, along with Egypt, Mesopotamia, and India, China has been called one of the cradles of civilization.

The earliest developments in China took place along the banks of the Hwang Ho about 3,500 years ago. In the years that followed, stories about China spread to other parts of the world. Hearing of the riches of the land, some people went to raid parts of China. As early as about 300 B.C. the Chinese built walls in the north to help keep out invaders. Over hundreds of years these walls were rebuilt and extended and finally became the Great Wall of China, about 1,700 miles in length.

Other men came to China for different reasons. Marco Polo set out from his home in Venice in A.D. 1271 for the long overland journey to Cathay, the name then given to China. Polo traveled with his father and uncle, who were merchants in search of trade. The three reached Peking in 1275 and were greeted by Kublai Khan, the Mongol warrior who was then ruling. After many years living at Peking and traveling in China for Kublai Khan, the Polos began their journey home in 1292. This time they went by sea, around India, up the Persian Gulf, and then by land to Venice.

They returned with silk cloth, bags of precious jewels, and other riches. Their tales of the wealth and way of life of the Chinese

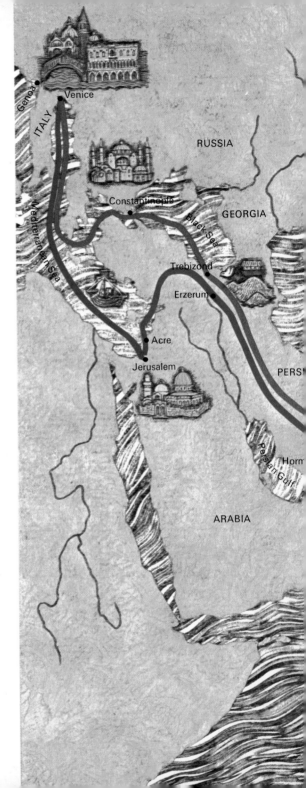

6

Marco Polo's itinerary 1271-1295

Venice to China 1271–1275

journeys in the service
of Kublai Khan

homeward journey 1292–1295

MONGOLIA

Shangtu

Peking

Gobi Desert

CHINA
(CATHAY)

Kanchow

Hangchow

Kashgar

AFGHANISTAN

TIBET

South China Sea

INDIA

Bay of Bengal

Arabian Sea

MALAY PENINSULA

CEYLON

SUMATRA

An area of recent factory development
is Lhasa, capital of the Tibetan
Autonomous Region

were of much interest to their friends in Venice, and many others in Europe learned of Marco Polo's travels from *The Book of Marco Polo* which was published later.

Traders from western countries were active especially in the coastal towns of China in the second half of the nineteenth century and early in the twentieth. But today few people are allowed to visit mainland China. In many ways this nation has become separate from the rest of the world.

The relief map shows that much of China's land frontier passes over high mountains. There are plateaus and basins and narrow mountain chains divided by steep-sided valleys. Few people live here; few people ever pass through. Nevertheless, much of Tibet is like this. Lhasa, the capital, is 11,800 feet above sea level. It is not surprising that Tibet is often called The Roof of the World.

Once an independent country, Tibet was occupied by the Chinese in the 1950s. Since then, wheeled vehicles have arrived in Tibet for the first time; road and rail links with

8

The agile yak, used as a pack animal
and as a source of rich milk and butter.
The hide and soft hair are also of use

China have been completed; and improvements have been made in what little farming, lumbering, and animal grazing there is. All the surplus produce from these improvements is exported to China.

But many areas of Tibet are very much as they were centuries ago. Most of the people are poor, and their homes are made of local stone, flat-roofed and with a room below for their animals. The yak, a long-haired ox, is very hardy, and it is quite common on the cold, dry plateaus of Tibet. The yak meat,

milk, hides, and hair are all of use. Tibetans are very fond of tea, which they flavor with the butter made from the yak's milk.

North of Tibet is the large province of Sinkiang, which is the other area of high western China. Sinkiang consists of two huge basins ringed by mountains and divided by the Tien Shan mountain chain. The Tarim basin is the one to the south. Except for the irrigated *oases* in surrounding valleys, the Tarim basin is mostly sandy desert, and it is here that nuclear missiles are tried out by the

9

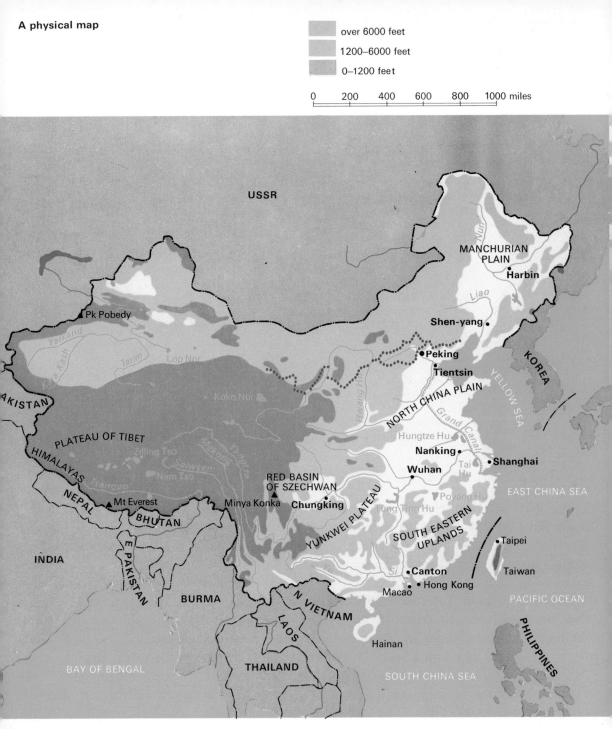

A physical map

over 6000 feet

1200–6000 feet

0–1200 feet

0   200   400   600   800   1000 miles

USSR

MANCHURIAN
PLAIN

Harbin

Nun

Liao

Shen-yang

Pk Pobedy

Yarkand

Kara Kash

Tarim

Lop Nor

Peking

Tientsin

KOREA

YELLOW
SEA

Koko Nor

Hwang Ho

NORTH CHINA PLAIN

Grand Canal

PAKISTAN

PLATEAU OF TIBET

HIMALAYAS

Zilling Tso

Nam Tso

Tsangpo

Salween

Mekong

Yangtze

Hungtze Hu

Nanking

Wuhan

Tai
Hu

Shanghai

EAST CHINA SEA

NEPAL

Mt Everest

BHUTAN

Minya Konka

RED BASIN
OF SZECHWAN

Chungking

Poyang Hu

Tung Ting Hu

YUNKWEI PLATEAU

SOUTH EASTERN
UPLANDS

Taipei

Taiwan

INDIA

E PAKISTAN

BURMA

N VIETNAM

LAOS

THAILAND

Si

Canton

Hong Kong

Macao

PACIFIC OCEAN

PHILIPPINES

Hainan

BAY OF BENGAL

SOUTH CHINA SEA

10

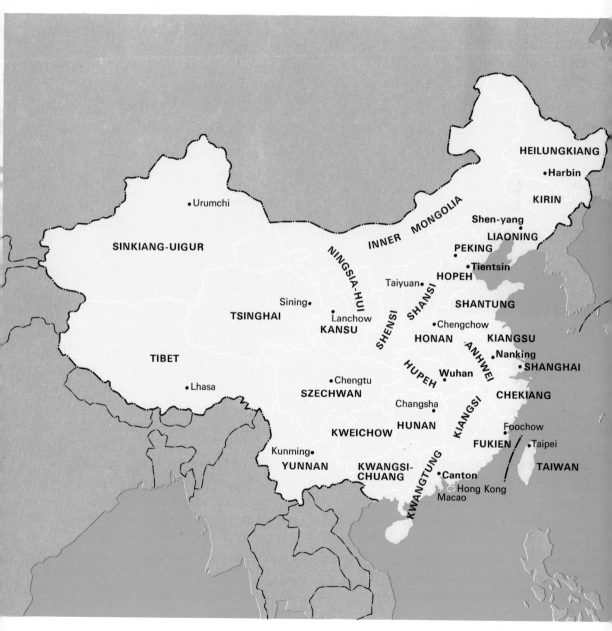

Chinese from their nuclear test center at Lop Nor, at the eastern end of the basin. The first Chinese satellite was launched not far from this isolated spot in 1970.

To the north is the Dzungaria basin, which is lower and better watered. *Nomads* move across the area with their horses, sheep, and cattle, but since 1950 settlers have come from the east to reclaim large areas of land for farming. An oil field was discovered at Karamai in 1955, the first of a number to be found in Dzungaria. This oil find has greatly helped China's industrial development, and the oil fields are now linked to Lanchow by pipeline and by rail. Large refineries have been built at Lanchow and at Tushantzu in Dzungaria.

Eastern China is much lower than these western areas of Tibet and Sinkiang. Even so, the east also has its basins, plateaus, and mountain chains, but the river valleys open out eastward to wide flat plains, and all the physical features are lower than those of the west.

The varied features of the east make a kind of checkerboard with their criss-cross pattern. Huge rivers carry millions of tons of *silt* eastward, and plains have been formed out of this silt, laid down during floods. Famine, floods, earthquakes, and civil wars have all been frequent in China's history; over the years millions of Chinese have thus lost their lives.

Left: the Taching Oil Refinery. The "thoughts of Mao Tse-tung" are often displayed in industrial, urban or rural scenes

Below: a group of peasant girls arrive for work on the dry terraced hillsides of Shansi Province

Winter rural scene along the banks of
the Yiho River in Tehpao County in
Kwangsi in south China

Right: a typical farming village

The Hwang Ho, or the Yellow River, of
northern China has been called China's
Sorrow because it has caused so much destruc-
tion during flooding. The yellow silt carried
by the river has covered the plains, so that in
the dry winter everywhere has this yellow
color. As the dry northerly winds are replaced
in the summer by the southeasterly *monsoon*
winds, the rain arrives and changes the color
to the green of growing crops.

Less and less irrigation is needed as one
moves southeastward, out of the dusty herds-

men's country of the west, toward the areas
watered by the summer rains.

China is a land of peasant farmers and
villages. No change of government has ever
changed this fact. The Chinese often build
their houses around, or to one side of, a
courtyard. The rough thatched houses of the
Hwang Ho plain are often packed tightly
together in large villages, which do not look
very prosperous, with uneven dirt tracks
twisting in and out. The farms of the Yangtze
river delta area are often mud-brick-walled

A graph showing the sharp rise in China's population in recent years. In 1970 there were 819 million people on the 3,691,502 square miles of the Chinese mainland

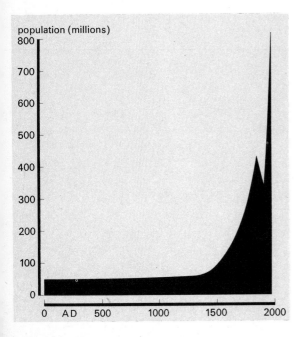

population (millions)

Japanese were defeated in 1945, the civil war continued until 1949, when the Communists, under Mao Tse-tung, drove the Nationalists out of the country to Taiwan (Formosa).

Since the Communists took command of the country the peasant farmer has seen many changes. In earlier times the average size of a farm was about 3½ acres, and few farmers owned their own land. The Communists changed this. Farmland was taken from the landlords and given to the peasants, and they were made to work together in small groups of six or seven households. Then larger holdings, co-operatives, were formed of thirty to forty households. These co-operatives were later grouped into even larger single farms called collectives.

In 1958 the Communists tried so many changes all at once that it was called The Year of the Great Leap Forward. The leap forward for the farmers was to have their collective farms made into yet larger single units, called communes. These averaged about 75 square miles in size, and each commune had several thousand households.

It was found that these large units were not easy to manage. For one thing, the transportation within the commune was difficult. So the communes were divided.

The new communes are centered on the old market towns, so the actual grouping of houses and other buildings has changed very little. The biggest changes have been the

and red-tile-roofed, and they often stand separate from each other rather than grouped into villages. But everywhere most men and women are busy obtaining as many crops as they can from the land, still using hoe and hand even though more machines are slowly appearing in the farming areas. The northern farmer has more draft animals to help him— mules, oxen, bullocks, and donkeys.

The greatest change in the countryside during the last hundred years has been the increase in the number of villages. The graph shows how the population has also increased.

In the 1930s and 1940s China had both civil war and war with Japan. Though the

16

The complex system of terracing in the highland area of Kansu Province

Preparing terraced paddy fields in the spring, Yunnan Province

View of a typical Chinese farmhouse

regrouping of the fields to make them larger, and the fact that all the farmers now work together in teams on each commune. Before each had his own small farm, often with tiny fields scattered in various places. Now the fields are much larger and are more regular in shape.

Only in the hilly areas are the fields still small and irregular. This is because the hillsides have been stepped into terraces, so that every part can be planted, often with rice under water which is held on the slopes by the stone walls at the edge of each terrace.

The larger fields make it easier to use the buffalo-drawn plow rather than the old hoe, and even the removal of the banks around the old, tiny fields has made an important difference by giving more land on which to sow seed.

The chief crops of north China are wheat, millet, *sorghum*, and cotton. In the south, especially along the Yangtze Kiang and Si Kiang valleys, rice is the main crop, while sugarcane, corn, and oranges are also produced. Tea, the popular Chinese beverage, is grown on the slopes between the Yangtze's southern tributaries.

Each commune decides how the men and women are to work. Though the plow and

Areas where four of the main crops are grown

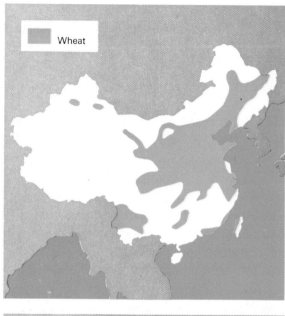
Wheat

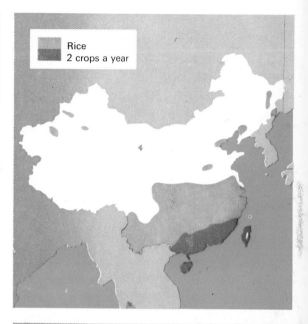
Rice
2 crops a year

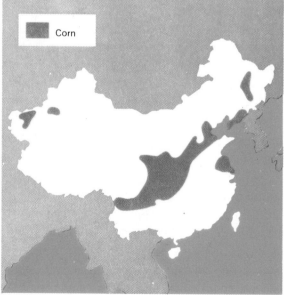
Corn

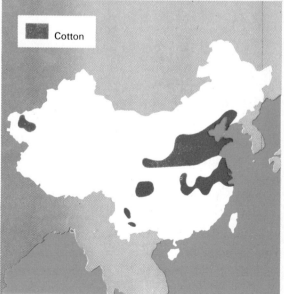
Cotton

19

some machines are now more widely used, much is still hand labor—digging, planting, weeding, and harvesting. Water stands in many of the fields, since this is needed for growing rice. Channels seem to run everywhere, delivering the water where it is needed as well as being useful for transportation. Trucks and cars are very scarce, but many farmers have their own boats.

In addition to working the land of the commune, each farmer is allowed his own small private plot. This is no more than a garden area alongside his house, but the Chinese farmers and their families work hard on this land to produce such things as vegetables, melons and tobacco. In the courtyard of the farmhouse is a hut for the farmer's own livestock (a water buffalo, pigs or perhaps sheep); hens also roam about the yard. There is a manure pit in the corner of the yard. Human manure is carefully stored here, and this is the chief fertilizer used on the fields.

The farmers' houses are often alongside the streams. Where there is a bridge there will sometimes be a group of shops: grocer, butcher, shoemaker, herb medicine shop. The local school and the temple will also be here.

Much in the village is built of wood: bridges, handcarts, hand flails for use at threshing time, treadmills where four or five men turn the wheel that lifts water up from one channel to another, so that it can reach each field. The hats that many wear are of bamboo. Often bamboo reeds are woven through a wooden framework to make the hut walls. These are then plastered with mud.

For most of the year there is work to do on the commune, and since much is done by hand the farmer has a hard life. The climate decides the busy seasons. It is not surprising that everyone should get excited about the festivals and celebrations that take place in between the busy periods. There are fewer religious celebrations than in the past, partly because the government has decided that these old customs waste too much time and partly because the Communists do not approve of religion. The main celebrations are now at New Year and for special Communist Party and army displays.

At New Year brightly colored costumes are worn, and fantastic dragon and lion masks cover the heads of those in the processions. At other times only the young Chinese seem to dress colorfully. As in Russia, many of the older children wear plainer clothes and, around their necks, the red scarves of the Young Pioneer Movement.

Soldiers in loose-fitting khaki uniforms parade in the towns and are also seen helping in the farming areas at busy times. Other men, and the women, wear white or blue open-necked cotton shirts over black slacks or, in the flooded rice fields, mud-covered shorts. Sandals are often worn. In towns, many people

Village work

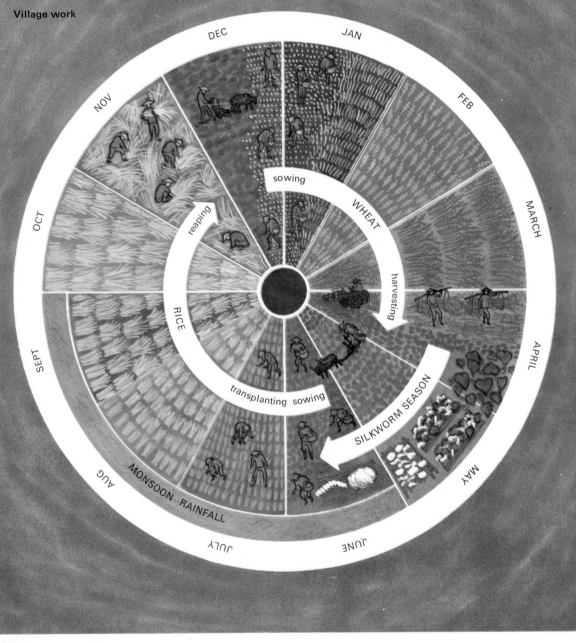

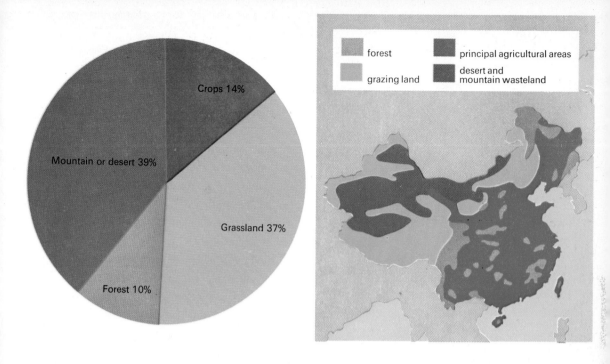

Crops 14%

Mountain or desert 39%

Grassland 37%

Forest 10%

forest

grazing land

principal agricultural areas

desert and mountain wasteland

wear blue cotton suits; in the colder areas suits of padded cotton are needed in the winter.

Many of the young people from the villages have moved to the towns and cities in search of work, but some have been sent back to help build up the labor force on the communes. Cottage or cooperative factory industries have also been encouraged in the farming areas. These industries produce agricultural machinery, fertilizers, clothing, shoes, and silk—from the worms that feed on the mulberry leaves collected from the trees growing alongside the streams or near the farmhouses. The women can find work in these industries, and the men also help at times when there is less to do in the fields.

As in the towns, there are day nurseries so that the women can be free to work all day. At some communes most meals are served centrally in dining halls.

Only about 12 percent of China is suitable for agriculture, so it is important that full use is made of all the farming land there is. With a quarter of the world's population but only 14 percent of the world's land area, the problem of producing enough food is a serious one.

In the 1950s the government named eight essentials for good farming, and attention was directed to the proper use of them: irrigation, fertilizers, soil improvement, close planting, plant protection from disease, the production of farming implements, seed improvement, and good administration.

Because of damage to crops and diseases brought to people, a campaign to reduce the numbers of rats, sparrows, flies, and *mosquitoes* was begun in the 1960s.

Left: a pumping station used for diverting some of the water of the Hwang Ho. Right: completed in 1960, this pumping station in the Tungchen People's Commune in Wenhsi County, Shansi Province, brings water to a dry upland area

Irrigation is very important in China. Rice is the chief crop, and this requires flooded fields in which to grow. In the dry north and west irrigation allows other crops such as wheat and corn to grow where there is not enough rainfall. Nearly half of China's farm-land is irrigated, and every year the irrigated area is increased.

The Hwang Ho Project has been started in an attempt to increase the irrigated areas around this river and its tributary valleys. Forty-six dams on the main river and twenty-four on the tributaries will hold back the water and store it. Already several of the dams are finished. The Sanmen Gorge Dam is one of the largest of these. The lake made behind it is almost 200 miles long.

In addition to providing water for irrigation, this river development plan will also help to check flooding, allow for the production of hydroelectric power at the dams, and provide long, deep channels for inland navigation.

The great quantity of silt carried down the Hwang Ho is a problem. The silt settles to the bottoms of the reservoirs, and if it is allowed to fill them up they become useless. Water can be drawn out at times to help wash out the silt. Now trees are being grown on some of the steep valley sides to hold the soil and prevent it from being washed into the rivers.

The Chinese say that they are turning China's Sorrow (the Hwang Ho) into China's Joy. On many occasions the Hwang Ho has

changed its course; sometimes the course of the river has been deliberately changed by the Chinese themselves—for example, to upset enemy forces. The mouth of the river is now north of the Shantung peninsula; at times in the past, though, the river has flowed into the Yellow Sea south of the peninsula.

Often in the past the river has flooded its plain. The plain is covered with yellow silt that was laid down during floods. A new supply of silt can help the farmer, but not when its arrival is uncontrolled and when the new silt is so thick that it covers crops, or when it arrives in a flood that washes away fields, farmhouses, and farm implements. Famine can result when crops are ruined; lives can be lost with serious floods.

Greater care is now being taken with many of China's rivers, and care is also taken in the hilly areas where terraced rice fields rise one above the other.

Eighty percent of the people live in the

Power resources

oil   ▲ thermo electric stations

natural gas   ○ hydroelectric stations   coalfields   —— oil pipe line

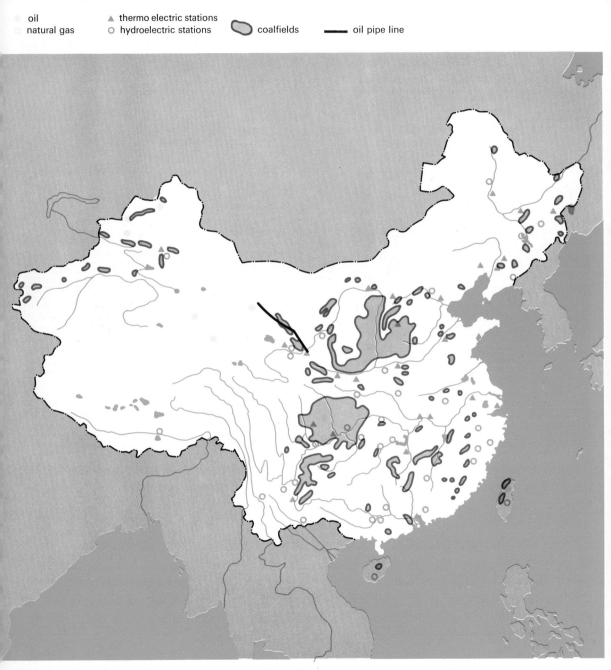

The Haichow opencut coal mine near Fusin in Lianing Province

farming villages, but the towns and cities are also important. The first Five Year Plan (1953–57) of the Communists aimed at improving the industrial development of the towns, and for this it was necessary to increase the production of steel, coal, oil, cement, and electricity.

Since then industrial expansion has continued. A map of 1958 showed eleven steel plants in China, mostly in the north and east; a 1970 map shows twenty-seven. Many of the new industrial sites are inland and are spread more evenly throughout the country.

China has great mineral wealth, and each year more of this is developed. Coal and iron ore, especially in the north and northeast, antimony and tungsten in the south, and tin in the south and southwest are all of great importance.

China is fortunate in having coal fields in many parts of the country, though not all are yet being worked. In some areas the coal can be mined from open pits. In Liaoning province, near Fushun, a city of over a million inhabitants, is the world's largest opencut coal mine.

Mechanized grabs lift the coal into the trucks of a cable railway. The rock covering the thick coal seams contains oil, and this is taken to a nearby oil refinery. Modern indus-

trial methods have been introduced, and the miners have up-to-date welfare services: public baths, libraries, clinics and social clubs.

China's largest coal reserves are in the province of Shansi and in the region of Inner Mongolia. There are different kinds of coal here, and the seams are fairly thick and easy to work. However it is only as road and rail links are extended that these areas can be opened up.

Not surprisingly, only the United States and Russia mine more coal than China.

The production of textiles is China's most important light industry. The clothes the Chinese wear are mostly made of cotton. Short *staple* cotton is grown as a summer crop over large areas of the flat Hwang Ho and Yangtze Kiang plains. Kiangsu province, north of the Yangtze delta, has the highest production.

There are cotton mills in many of the towns and cities along the Hwang and Yangtze valleys. One such city is Wuhan, the collective name given to the three adjoining cities of Hankow, Hanyang, and Wuchang. In the last few years modern new mills have been added to the older ones here. Spinning, weaving, and dyeing all take place.

The iron and steel industry of Wuhan is also important. The raw materials—coal, iron ore, and limestone—are all near at hand, as is the river for water supply and transportation.

28

Left: rows of blast furnaces at the Anhwei iron and steel plant

Below: old and new type coke ovens at the Wuhan iron and steel plant

Wuhan is in the center of eastern China, the half where most of the people live. And dividing this half, north to south, is the main railway from Peking to Canton. The trains had to be ferried across the Yangtze at Wuhan until 1957 when, at a point 1,250 yards across, a bridge was completed. This spectacular bridge has two levels: a six-lane road above and a double-track railway below.

Wuhan is also in the center of the Middle Basin of the Yangtze Kiang. The river enters this broad plain from a gorge farther west. Within the plain are some of the richest farming areas in China, and they are densely populated. In Wuhan itself there are over two and a half million people.

West of the Yangtze Gorges is the Red Basin of Szechwan, so called because of the

The railway bridge across the Yangtze at Nanking

Below right: a cotton mill in the Wuhan area

color of the soil. The surprisingly mild winters
and hot summers here, together with adequate
rainfall and irrigation systems, make it a rich
agricultural area. A great variety of crops are
grown: tea, corn and sugarcane, for example,
though rice is the chief summer crop and
wheat the chief winter crop.

The Red Basin is also developing industries,
based upon local supplies of coal, oil, salt and
iron ore.

The waterways of China have always been
most important for transportation, and the
Yangtze Kiang and its tributaries form the
largest network. Only in the Yangtze Gorges is
the river difficult, even dangerous, for boats.

Large vessels reach Wuhan; *junks* are everywhere. As well as acting as the taxis of the
river for both people and commodities (tea,
rice, vegetable oils, tobacco, etc.), the junks
serve as homes for families.

As the Yangtze flows eastward and its
channel widens, larger vessels and more junks
are to be seen using this highway. After passing
the old capital Nanking, an industrial and
trading city of almost three million people, the
river widens again in its delta area, and here,
standing some distance up a tributary creek, is
the great city of Shanghai. This is the largest
city in China and has over ten million
inhabitants.

Shanghai grew as a trade center in China
for foreign nations. This lasted for a hundred
years, and though these traders have now all
gone, their western-style buildings remain.
Manufacturing came with the trade, and for
years this has been China's most important
textile town.

Some shipping still exists, but Shanghai is
no longer one of the leading world ports.
Nevertheless its growth has continued. The
new areas of housing built by the present
Communist government look very much like
the apartment blocks they have built in other
Chinese cities, and very much like those in
Russia. These long, five-story-high blocks give
one- or two-room homes for the extra thousands by which the city's population increases
each year.

Transportation on the Yangtze

Industrial and mineral resources

- antimony
- tungsten
- tin
- aluminum
- ◆ manganese
- ○ copper
- ▼ lead/zinc
- ■ iron ore
- ○ silk
- ▲ ship building
- ▣ chemical manufacture
- ───── main highways
- ───── principal railways
- ⊙ principal airports

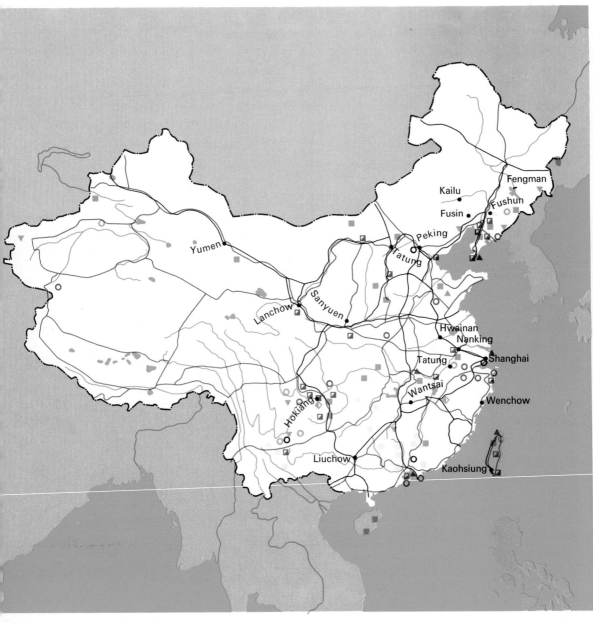

Kailu
Fengman
Fusin
Fushun
Peking
Tatung
Yumen
Sanyuen
Lanchow
Hwainan
Nanking
Tatung
Shanghai
Wantsai
Wenchow
Hokiang
Liuchow
Kaohsiung

Shanghai on the Huang Pu, tributary of
the Yangtze Kiang

One of the four halls of the Imperial Palace in what was the "Forbidden City" within Peking. The halls are now museums open to the public

Right: lamas of the Yuan-chao Temple at Wu-tai-shan, one of the four Chinese mountains sacred to Buddhism

Most of China's cities still have some beautiful old buildings. The thick, high walls built for defense have sometimes been pulled down —in Wuchang (part of Wuhan) for example, conveniently providing room for a broad, new road that circles the city. Palaces of former emperors remain in some of the cities that have at different times served as China's capital. The religions of China's people have provided most of the richly decorated and distinctly designed buildings.

Buddhist temples and *pagodas*, often very beautiful and colorful, can be seen in many of the countries of southeast Asia. Buddhism came from India to China in A.D. 67. This religion teaches that man must try to improve himself and that he is born again and again after death until he is fully perfect. Buddhists believe that the universe changes and that what man does may upset the universe but cannot alter its laws. Buddhists also believe in living peacefully.

Confucius (about 551 to 479 B.C.) was a great Chinese thinker and teacher. He tried to

36

These three religions have existed together in China for hundreds of years, and many Chinese have accepted some of each or all of each of the religions. But these ways of thinking are not accepted by the Communists. Religion of any kind is discouraged by the government.

Many of the temples in Peking, China's present capital city, have been turned into museums. The massive Imperial Palace of the early emperors is also now a museum. In many museums the story of the rise of Communism in China is told. These beautiful old buildings are visited by thousands each year. In contrast, most new buildings are boxlike gray concrete masses and not at all attractive.

Except in the old part of Peking, the streets are wide and tree-lined and are kept tidy and clean. There are buses but few private cars. There are many bicycles, even though these are very expensive. Communist slogans, such as "Long Live the Communist Party of China," are painted on huge boards or flags for all to see. Pictures of Mao Tse-tung, Chairman of the Central Committee of the Chinese Communist Party, are everywhere, just as common as Lenin's picture is in Moscow. The aim is to get rid of old thinking, customs, and habits.

A city of six million people, Peking has always been a cultural and trading center rather than an industrial city. However, some industries have grown up in the suburban

discover what it meant to be good, and he believed that what mattered most in life were good relationships, especially within each family. Followers of this teaching are called Confucianists.

Taoism is another Chinese religion. Many believe that this religion began from the teachings of Lao-tze (604 to 500 B.C.), who said that goodness came from living a simple life and by accepting all that happened without question.

38

areas. As with industry everywhere in China, it is controlled by the state.

Today Peking's chief function is to act as the center from which the strong government control extends over all The People's Republic of China.

Northeast of Peking is the area once known as Manchuria. In the past both Russia and Japan have occupied this area. Though the long winters here are very cold, the summers are warm; vast areas are flat plain, and there is usually sufficient rainfall for a good summer crop of *kaoliang*, *soybean*, sugar beet, or wheat on the large communes and state farms. The mountains around are wooded with pine, larch, and fir. Much of China's timber comes from this area.

With the industrial development at places like Anshan and Fushun, it is not surprising that Manchuria has become a major population growth area. The steel for the Yangtze Bridge at Wuhan came from the modern steel

39

plant at Anshan. Many more Chinese are likely to move out from the crowded center of the country and continue the development of the rich natural resources of Manchuria.

In the 1940s the defeated Nationalist Chinese fled to the island of Taiwan (Formosa), and their leader, General Chiang Kai-shek, made Taipei their capital. This is how the two Chinas of today came into being.

With 12,500,000 inhabitants to feed, the farmers of Taiwan nevertheless manage to produce enough food for them as well as some for export. Two crops of rice are grown each year; sugarcane is the most important export crop. Fishing also produces a rich supply of food, just as it does for mainland China.

Several industries have been developed, especially in the north of the island. Plastics, bicycles, plate glass, and cotton textiles are some of the chief products.

Left: a cucumber market. Right: old
and new forms of transportation and
buildings in Taipei, capital of Taiwan
(Formosa)

Spread over several islands and onto mainland China southeast of the industrial port of Canton is the small British colony of Hong Kong. Four million people are jammed into this tiny area, and housing is a major problem. As in Canton, many families still live in makeshift huts or on the thousands of small fishing boats, though huge apartment blocks have been built in many areas. Countless refugees have arrived in Hong Kong since the Communists took control of China.

Jobs are provided for many by the numerous light industries and the trade connected with this large port.

The United Kingdom's 99-year lease of Hong Kong from China began in 1898. It will be interesting to see what happens when the lease ends. At present Hong Kong serves as a window from which westerners can look into China. It also serves as an outlet for Chinese goods and ideas, as well as people, to the Western world.

42

Recently harvested paddy fields in the
New Territories, Kowloon Peninsula

The Great Wall of China

China is certainly becoming a very powerful nation, and it seems that the Chinese government has decided to spread its Communist ideas to other parts of the world. Since the Second World War, China has been active in many conflicts in its neighboring states, notably in Korea, Vietnam, Cambodia, Taiwan, and India. Tibet was occupied by China in 1959. There have been boundary disputes with Russia, India, and Pakistan. Farther afield, in Africa for example, China has tried to influence other nations, partly by sending money and men to some states.

Tight control keeps peace in China itself and keeps foreign visitors out. Other nations of the world watch with great interest and some concern the future of this rapidly growing country.

45

Some questions to choose from

1. Describe the physical features of the frontier areas between China and each of her neighbors.

2. Under the headings rainfall, temperature, crops and building materials list some of the differences between north and south China.

3. Describe the different kinds of terraces shown in the three pictures on pages 13 and 17.

4. Give possible reasons why each of the "eight essentials for good farming" (see page 23) was listed by the Chinese government.

5. In what ways can China help to overcome the various natural disasters which have been frequent in her history?

6. Draw a map to show Hong Kong's location and its links with trade routes.

7. What factors have helped recent industrial growth in China?

8. Look at the pictures on pages 27, 28 and 29 and then list some of the old and new methods of working that you can see.

9. In what different ways are goods transported from place to place in China?

10. Which is the better location for China's capital city, Peking or Nanking? Give your reasons.

Difficult words :

junks—wooden sailing craft, flat-bottomed, and with broad, high stern and bow.

kaoliang—a tall plant with a big, bushy grain head; each grain is about the size of a split pea; the long stalks are used for roofing, the threshed heads are used in northern China for broom heads.

monsoon—a wind which changes its direction seasonally. Caused by the seasonal differences of temperature between land and sea areas.

mosquitoes—kinds of gnats, the female of which feeds on the blood of animals. (The female Anopheles mosquito carries malaria.)

nomads—people who often change their dwelling place.

oases—fertile watered areas in the midst of a desert.

pagodas—sacred buildings, usually towers built using pyramid forms.

silt—mud deposited by water.

sorghum—a grain-producing tropical grass.

soybean—a plant with white or purple flowers from which seed pods develop; the plant is good animal feed, the beans make a rich food for man or animals.

staple—the thread of wool, cotton, or flax.

Some Chinese words

ho	river
hwang	yellow
kang (or kong)	port
kiang	river
king	capital
ling (or shan)	mountain
nan	south
nor (or tso)	lake
pei (or peh)	north
si (or hsi)	west
tung	east

Printed in Great Britain

J